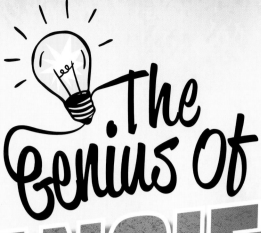

The Genius Of THE ANCIENT EGYPTIANS

INNOVATIONS FROM PAST CIVILIZATIONS

SONYA NEWLAND

CRABTREE
PUBLISHING COMPANY
WWW.CRABTREEBOOKS.COM

CRABTREE
PUBLISHING COMPANY
WWW.CRABTREEBOOKS.COM

Published in Canada
Crabtree Publishing
616 Welland Avenue
St. Catharines, ON
L2M 5V6

Published in the United States
Crabtree Publishing
PMB 59051
350 Fifth Ave, 59th Floor
New York, NY 10118

Published in 2020 by Crabtree Publishing Company

First published in Great Britain in 2019 by The Watts Publishing Group
Copyright © The Watts Publishing Group 2019

Author: Sonya Newland

Editorial director: Kathy Middleton

Editors: Sonya Newland, Petrice Custance

Proofreader: Melissa Boyce

Series Designer: Rocket Design (East Anglia) Ltd

Designer: Steve Mead

Prepress technician: Tammy McGarr

Print coordinator: Katherine Berti

Consultant: Philip Parker

Photo credits:
Alamy: Juergen Ritterbach 7t, Granger Historical Picture Archive 11l, 17, Peter Horree 11r, dieKleinert 21b, Barry Iverson 26; Ron Dixon: 12; Getty Images: Print Collector 14, DEA Picture Library 15, 21t, DEA / G. DAGLI ORTI 20, 24, Science & Society Picture Library 25, 28, 29r; iStock: WitR Cover, 6, 8, TerryJLawrence 5, 18, FunnyGirl 7b, LexyLovesArt 9r, Tjanze 10, Flory 13b, prill 16, shishic 19, ttatty 22, Maciek67 27b; Shutterstock: Anton_Ivanov 9l, Kostyantyn Ivanyshen 13t, francesco de marco 23, mountainpix 27t, Niall O'Donoghue 29l; White-Thomson Publishing: 4.

All design elements from Shutterstock.

Printed in the U.S.A./072019/CG20190501

Library and Archives Canada Cataloguing in Publication

Title: The genius of the ancient Egyptians / Sonya Newland.
Names: Newland, Sonya, author.
Series: Genius of the ancients.
Description: Series statement: The genius of the ancients | Includes index.
Identifiers: Canadiana (print) 20190108185 | Canadiana (ebook) 20190108193 | ISBN 9780778765714 (hardcover) | ISBN 9780778765912 (softcover) | ISBN 9781427123886 (HTML)
Subjects: LCSH: Egypt—Civilization—To 332 B.C.—Juvenile literature. | LCSH: Technological innovations—Egypt—History—To 1500—Juvenile literature.
Classification: LCC DT61 .N49 2019 | DDC j932—dc23

Library of Congress Cataloging-in-Publication Data

Names: Newland, Sonya, author.
Title: The genius of the ancient Egyptians / Sonya Newland.
Description: New York, New York : Crabtree Publishing Company; 2020. Series: The genius of the ancients
Identifiers: LCCN 2019014232 (print) | LCCN 2019017529 (ebook) | ISBN 9781427123886 (Electronic) | ISBN 9780778765714 (hardcover) | ISBN 9780778765912 (pbk.)
Subjects: LCSH: Egypt--Civilization--To 332 B.C.--Juvenile literature.
Classification: LCC DT61 (ebook) | LCC DT61 .N45 2020 (print) | DDC 609/.32--dc23
LC record available at https://lccn.loc.gov/2019014232

CONTENTS

THE ANCIENT EGYPTIANS

Who were the Egyptians?

People began to live along the banks of the Nile River in Egypt around 9,000 years ago. As time passed, these small groups of hunters and fishers began to settle and grow crops. In turn, these farming communities grew into villages and towns. Systems of trade developed, and by 3000 B.C.E., a **civilization** had been established that would become one of the greatest in the world.

Egyptian kingdoms

Ancient Egyptian history is generally divided into three kingdoms: the Old Kingdom (2686–2181 B.C.E.), the Middle Kingdom (2050–1786 B.C.E.), and the New Kingdom (1567–1085 B.C.E.). The Egyptian civilization flourished during the years of these kingdoms. The time periods between the kingdoms were years of weaker rule, when there was fighting and unrest in Egypt.

This map shows the area of ancient Egypt along with some of the key sites the Egyptians built along the Nile River.

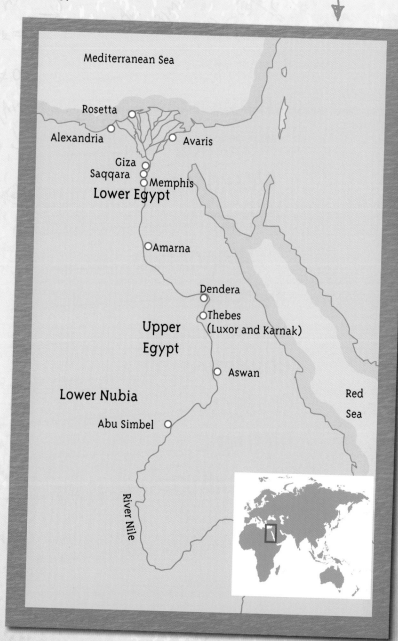

Powerful leaders

The rulers of Egypt were called **pharaohs**. They showed their power and wealth by building impressive temples and pyramids to honor themselves and the many gods they worshiped. For more than 2,500 years, great pharaohs such as Khufu, Hatshepsut, and Rameses II ruled over a **prosperous** land.

Wall paintings such as this one from the tomb of Setau, named for a high-ranking Egyptian, reveal much about the lifestyle and beliefs of the ancient Egyptians.

What happened?

Throughout this time, the Egyptians sometimes had to fight neighboring peoples, such as the Nubians and the Assyrians. But Egypt's desert location kept it fairly safe from invaders and, for the most part, life there went on the same for centuries. Eventually, in 30 B.C.E., this great civilization fell under the control of the Romans.

The ancient Egyptians left behind a huge legacy of information. This is contained in many different **artifacts**, from palaces and temples to paintings, **hieroglyphics** (see pages 10–11), and even dead bodies!

PYRAMIDS

The ancient Egyptians are most famous for building the pyramids. More than 100 of these structures have been found in Egypt. But in the days before cranes or any other modern building equipment, how were the Egyptians able to construct such mighty monuments?

What were the pyramids?

Pyramids were huge tombs, built as the final resting place for pharaohs or other important people. Inside were many different rooms, including storerooms and bedrooms. The interior walls were beautifully decorated with paintings, or engraved with prayers and stories.

The pyramid shape represented the Sun's rays shining down from the sky.

WOW!

The largest pyramid, the Great Pyramid of Giza, was built for the pharaoh Khufu. When completed in 2560 B.C.E., it stood more than 480 feet (146 m) high and consisted of around 2.3 million blocks of stone.

6

Amazing architects

Ancient Egyptian **architects** chose the position of a pyramid carefully. For example, they might make sure that it lined up with the sunrise on a certain day of the year. They also designed the pyramid to protect both the pharaoh's body and the treasure inside the tomb. Fake entrances were included to fool robbers. Inside was a maze of passageways, false doors, and litter-filled rooms to confuse anyone who managed to get in.

A corridor inside the tomb of two royal servants, Niankhkhnum and Khnumhotep, located in Saqqara.

Building the pyramids

Stone for the pyramids mostly came from a nearby **quarry**. The huge blocks were cut and then hauled on sleds across the desert. Once at the building site, the blocks were added to the pyramid using a system of ramps made of mud. As the pyramid got higher, the ramps were lengthened and widened to keep them stable. To fill the gaps and smooth the surface, finishing blocks made of limestone were added.

Very early pyramids were built with stepped sides.

TEMPLES

Like the pyramids, Egyptian temples were incredible building achievements. Nothing in the ancient world could compare with these great monuments to the pharaohs and the gods.

Four huge statues guard the entrance to the rock-carved temple at Abu Simbel.

Religion in Egypt

Religion was very important to the ancient Egyptians, and they worshiped many gods. They believed that a temple was the home of the god or goddess it was dedicated to, so it was a very important place. Priests performed special ceremonies and **rituals** to honor the gods and keep them happy. People brought **offerings** to temples to be made to the gods.

WOW!

The temple complex at Karnak is one of the biggest religious sites ever built. This city of temples covers an area larger than 180 football fields!

8

Temples—outside and in

Some temples, such as the temples at Luxor, were built from stone blocks. Others, such as those at Abu Simbel, were carved out of solid rock. Inside the temple were huge stone pillars to support the heavy roof. The walls were covered with carvings and paintings. The art often told tales of the pharaohs' great victories, and showed them in the company of the gods.

This chamber in Rameses II's temple at Abu Simbel contains a statue of the goddess Hathor.

Obelisks

Obelisks were tall, four-sided pillars that were placed in pairs on either side of the entrance to a temple. They narrowed from a wide base to a pyramid shape at the top. An obelisk was usually created from a single, huge piece of granite, and they were enormously heavy. No one knows exactly how the Egyptians raised them up once they had been carved!

(((BRAIN WAVE)))

To avoid hauling heavy stone obelisks a long way, they were usually created at quarries on the banks of the Nile River. Specially built boats carried the obelisks along the river to the temple site.

Obelisks were associated with the Sun god Ra. The ancient Egyptians believed that he existed within these stone pillars.

WRITING

The ancient Egyptians wanted to record important events in their world. To do this, they became one of the first civilizations to develop their language into a form of writing. In fact, the amazing Egyptians created several systems of writing, including hieroglyphics and **hieratic**.

★GENIUS★
WRITTEN COMMUNICATION

Picture writing

At first, the Egyptians used pictures to represent objects. As this form of writing developed, it began to include more **abstract** shapes, which represented certain sounds. Having these additional symbols meant that people could write down such things as names and ideas. These pictures and symbols are known as hieroglyphics, which comes from the Greek word for "**sacred** carving."

WOW!

The ancient Egyptian writing system contained more than 700 main hieroglyphics.

The name of a royal person was written in an oval with a line at one end, called a cartouche. This cartouche is from a temple at Luxor.

Joining things up

Alongside hieroglyphics, the Egyptians developed a cursive, or joined-up, form of writing called hieratic. The word means "priestly writing" and it was called this because it was mainly used for religious texts. Hieratic was much quicker to write than hieroglyphics, especially as it was usually written in ink on **papyrus** (see pages 12–13) rather than carved on stone.

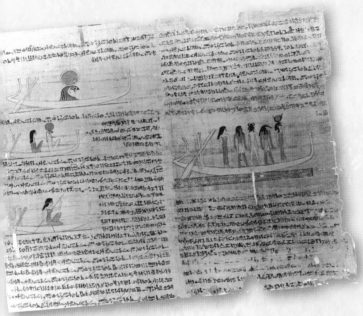

Unlike hieroglyphics, which could be written in rows or columns, hieratic was always written in rows and read from right to left.

Ancient graffiti

Examples of ancient writing can be seen all over Egypt. Hieroglyphics are carved onto pillars, columns, and obelisks, as well as the stone walls of pyramids and temples. They recount the history of Egypt and its people by recording great battles, political events, prayers to the gods, and praise for the pharaohs.

TEST of TIME

For many years, no one could read hieroglyphics. The discovery of the Rosetta Stone in 1799 changed that. On this stone was the same piece of text written in hieroglyphics, a later Egyptian writing called Demotic, and ancient Greek. By comparing the three, experts figured out what different hieroglyphics meant.

The text on the Rosetta Stone is an official announcement honoring the pharaoh Ptolemy V.

PAPYRUS

Before the Egyptians created papyrus sheets, people wrote on tablets made of stone or clay, or on pieces of wood or animal skin. When other civilizations discovered the Egyptians' clever invention, it caused a writing revolution.

GENIUS ★ WRITING PAPER

Making paper

Papyrus is a tall plant that grows in the marshy areas along the banks of the Nile. Inside the papyrus stalk is a strong, fibrous material that can be peeled into strips using a sharp tool. To make papyrus sheets, strips from the stalk were laid out in two layers, one across the other. They were then pressed and dried. Once dried, the sheets were often joined together to create longer scrolls.

TEST OF TIME

The English word paper has its origins in *pápuros*, which is the word the ancient Greeks used for Egyptian papyrus.

MAKING PAPYRUS SHEETS

1. The outer green skin was sliced off the stem.

2. Thin slices of the **pith** inside the papyrus stem were placed in two layers, one on top of the other.

3. The layers were beaten with a **mallet** to help the fibers bond together.

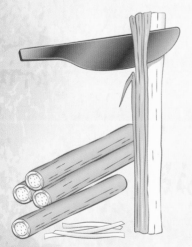

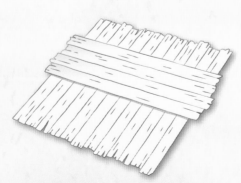

Priceless papyrus

For 3,000 years, papyrus was very valuable in the ancient world. Everyone wanted it, and the Egyptians **exported** it all over the Mediterranean region. This trade was very important to Egypt. To ensure that other civilizations could not make it for themselves, the Egyptians kept the method of making papyrus a closely guarded secret.

papyrus plants

(((**BRAIN WAVE**)))

The Egyptians needed something they could use to write on papyrus sheets. They created a type of black ink out of vegetable gum, beeswax, and soot. To make different colors, they replaced the soot with a different ingredient. For example, a type of clay called ocher was used to make a reddish color.

Copies of the Egyptian **Book of the Dead**, a book of spells, were written on papyrus scrolls.

FARMING METHODS

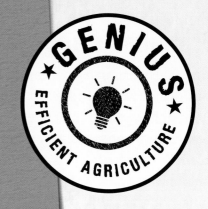

Most ordinary Egyptians were farmers, so it's not surprising that they invented many things that helped them farm more efficiently.

The old-fashioned way

One of the most important jobs for a farmer was breaking up the soil to make it ready to plant crops. Most ancient civilizations, including the Egyptians, used hand plows to prepare the soil. Hand plows had to be small and light so farmers could carry them. Hand plowing was slow, backbreaking work.

Animal power

The Egyptians realized that plowing would be much easier if they used animals. So, they designed a plow that could be attached to oxen. The oxen could pull a plow through the earth much more quickly than a human could. Workers would follow behind the plow, breaking up large chunks of soil with hoes. Seeds were then planted in the **furrows** the plow created.

This wooden model dating from 2040 to 1750 B.C.E. shows an Egyptian farmer with his ox-drawn plow.

Tools of the trade

Both the Egyptians and the Mesopotamians in western Asia are believed to have invented the sickle at about the same time. A sickle was a farming tool with a curved blade, usually made from **flint**, which was attached to a wooden handle. At **harvest** time, farmers moved through their fields, swinging the sickle from side to side to cut down crops such as wheat and barley. The Egyptians were also among the first to make other farming equipment, such as hoes and rakes. They also made winnowing baskets which were used to separate grain from **chaff**. The mixture was thrown in the air, the wind blew away the chaff, and the grains were caught in the basket.

This wall painting from a tomb in Thebes shows scenes of harvesting crops.

15

IRRIGATION

In the dry desert, it was essential to find ways of getting water to fields for crops to grow. The Egyptians came up with such ingenious **irrigation** methods that other **cultures**, including the ancient Greeks and Romans, began using them.

GENIUS
★ TRANSPORTING WATER ★

The vital Nile

Every year, rains to the south caused the Nile River in Egypt to flood. This was crucial to ancient Egyptian agriculture because when the floodwater **receded**, it left behind a rich soil that was perfect for growing crops. Good soil was important, but crops also needed to be watered as they were growing. The ancient Egyptians had to find ways of getting water to fields located farther away from the Nile.

(((**BRAIN WAVE**)))

To keep the floodwater near their fields, the Egyptians built **reservoirs** out of mud bricks. These trapped the water as it receded.

The Nile flood is still an important event for the Egyptians. It is celebrated by a festival in August every year.

Canals

To control the flow of water, farmers created canals by digging trenches from the river all the way to their fields. These canals also filled up during the flood, providing a store of water for the dry season. However, there was still a problem. How could the farmers lift the water out of the canals to use on their fields? They solved this problem with a device called a shadoof.

The shadoof

A shadoof consisted of a long pole balanced on a crossbeam. A bucket was attached to a rope at one end, and at the shorter end was a **counterweight**. The farmer pulled on the rope to lower the bucket into the canal. When the bucket was full of water, the farmer raised it again by pulling on the counterweight. The pole could be swung around, allowing water to be poured wherever it was needed.

WOW!

Sometimes a series of shadoofs were mounted one above the other. This system allowed water to be raised to higher levels in stages.

This painting from a tomb of the sculptor Ipuy at Luxor shows a farmer using a shadoof.

counterweight

bucket

CALENDARS

The annual flooding of the Nile River was essential to the rhythm of life in ancient Egypt. To know when the floods would take place, and to plan their farming year, the Egyptians needed an accurate calendar.

GENIUS
★ YEAR-LONG CALENDAR ★

Eyes to the sky

The pattern of life in ancient Egypt was based on the natural cycles of the Sun and the Moon. The Egyptians used a lunar calendar, based on the phases of the Moon, to keep track of important religious festivals and events. However, they needed to measure everyday life in a different way. The star they called Sopdet, now known as Sirius, appeared in the eastern sky every year at the same time as the flooding of the Nile River. They used this event as the basis for a solar calendar.

The Dendera Zodiac is an ancient Egyptian temple carving showing the pattern of **constellations** in the night sky.

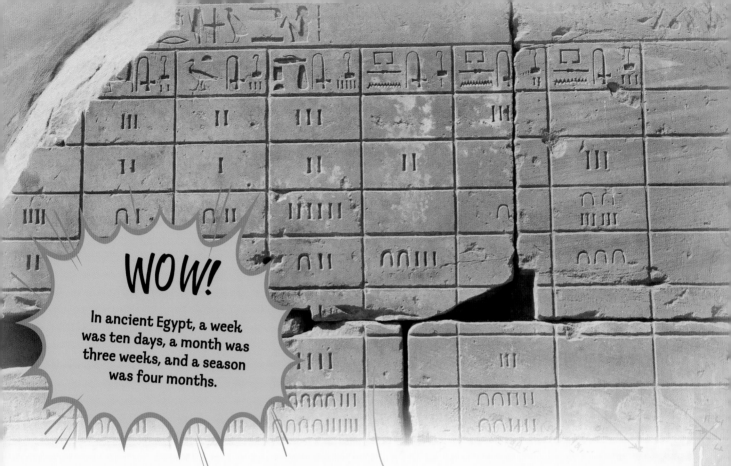

WOW!

In ancient Egypt, a week was ten days, a month was three weeks, and a season was four months.

This calendar is carved on the wall of a temple in the complex at Karnak.

Three seasons

Today, we have four seasons. In ancient Egypt, life was so closely tied to farming that they divided the year into three seasons. These seasons corresponded to important periods in the farming year: **inundation** (the period when the Nile River flooded), growing, and harvest. Each season was made up of four months of 30 days. This calendar added up to 360 days.

The 365-day calendar

The Egyptians eventually recognized their solar year was too short because the months were no longer matching up with the seasons. To fix this, they added five extra days between harvest and inundation. These days became religious holidays, set aside to honor the birthdays of different gods.

TEST OF TIME

A year is actually 365 and one-quarter days long. The Egyptians had not accounted for the fraction, so the calendar became increasingly inaccurate. In 238 B.C.E., Ptolemy III added an extra day every four years. We still use this system today, known as a leap year, where an extra day is added to February every four years.

CLOCKS

Calendars helped the ancient Egyptians keep track of annual events, but they also wanted to keep accurate time throughout the day. This was particularly important for priests and the regular performance of religious ceremonies.

Sunshine and shadow

One of the first methods the ancient Egyptians used to measure time was a shadow clock. The Sun struck the shadow clock on a **gnomon**. Based on the length and position of the shadow cast by the gnomon, people could tell the time of day.

Over time, the Egyptians developed shadow clocks into more sophisticated sundials. An Egyptian sundial had twelve lines marked on the base, radiating from the center. The Egyptians knew what time of day it was by which line the shadow fell on.

gnomon

sundial

Time drips by

Using a sundial was all very well on a bright sunny day, but how did the ancient Egyptians tell the time at night or when it was overcast? They used a water clock. This was usually a stone bowl or a cone-shaped vessel. It had a tiny hole in the bottom and evenly spaced markings up the inside. The container was filled with water, which dripped out through the hole at a constant rate, so the passing of time could be measured by looking at the water level against the markings.

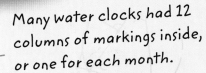
Many water clocks had 12 columns of markings inside, or one for each month.

BRAIN WAVE

The ancient Egyptians used obelisks as a type of sundial. They noted how the shadow moved around the surface of the obelisk throughout the course of the day. From this they could figure out the longest and shortest days of the year.

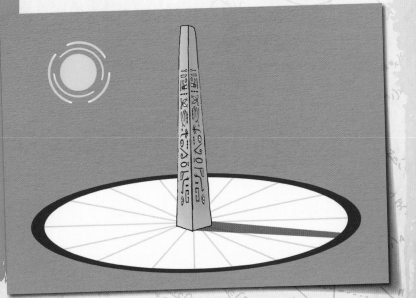

21

MUMMIFICATION

GENIUS ★
PRESERVING BODIES

We know a lot about the kinds of medical problems that the ancient Egyptians suffered from. This is largely thanks to their expertise in **preserving** the bodies of the dead. The ritual of **mummification** was extremely important in Egyptian society.

Essentials for the afterlife

The ancient Egyptians believed that for someone to reach the afterlife, their body had to be preserved. So, the bodies of wealthy, important people were mummified. Afterward, the body was placed in a tomb with all the things the person might need in the next life, including clothes, jewelry, household items, and food. Ordinary people were simply buried in the desert, where the dry sand often preserved their bodies naturally.

The ancient Egyptians believed that Anubis, the god of the dead, weighed someone's heart when they died. This was done to judge whether they could pass into the afterlife. In this scene from the Book of the Dead, Anubis is on the left and in the middle.

Making a mummy

First the body was washed, to purify it for the afterlife. Then all the organs except the heart were removed from the body. Most of the organs were preserved in special containers which were buried with the person.

Drying out

The body was filled with a type of stuffing and covered with a natural salt called natron. This dried out the body. It was left for 40 to 50 days, after which the stuffing was removed and replaced with either cloth or sawdust. Bandages were wound around the body before it was placed in a stone coffin called a sarcophagus.

(((BRAIN WAVE)))

Priests did not want to cut open the skull of a deceased person. To remove the brain, they inserted a special hook up the nose, and pulled the brain out through the nasal passage. Unlike most organs, the brain was not preserved.

Some bodies have been so well preserved that even thousands of years later they are recognizably human.

WOW!

It took about 70 days to preserve a body. During the process of mummification, the priest wore a mask which represented the god Anubis.

MEDICINE

Just like people today, the Egyptians had accidents and caught diseases. Not only did they discover several new ways of treating illnesses, they were also the **pioneers** of a number of different surgical procedures.

★ GENIUS ★
LIFE-SAVING MEDICINE

Herbal medicine

The ancient Egyptians suffered from a whole range of diseases, including arthritis, **tuberculosis**, and tooth decay. Like many ancient civilizations, they turned to nature to treat almost all of these ailments. They made medicine from plants and herbs, often mixed with wine.

This wall painting from a tomb at Saqqara shows precious ointment being transported in a jar.

WOW!

When doctors could not find any obvious cause of an illness, they would say it was caused by spirits. Spells and magic potions were used to try and drive these evildoers away.

Healing honey

Honey was a key ingredient in many Egyptian treatments. Today we know that honey has **antibacterial** properties, and the ancient Egyptians noticed that putting honey on wounds prevented or cured infection. They also made a medicine out of honey mixed with wine and milk.

Surgical advances

The ancient Egyptians were the first people to set bones when they had been broken, to help them heal properly. They also performed advanced operations, such as brain surgery and **cesarean sections** to deliver babies. Archaeologists have even found **prosthetic** body parts, such as toes made out of wood. Many surgical instruments have been discovered, including scalpels, needles for sewing up wounds, scissors, and forceps.

TEST of TIME

A papyrus document shows that the ancient Egyptians used many of the same things we use today for treating wounds. It mentions lint, bandages, and thread for stitches.

These knives may have been used during surgery or for hooking organs out of the body during the process of mummification.

25

DENTAL CARE

There were no dentists in ancient Egypt, and the Egyptians had to suffer through dental problems such as cavities and **abscesses**. To limit these problems, they tried to keep their teeth clean in several ways.

Mummies discovered in ancient Egypt often show signs of worn teeth and mouth diseases.

A recipe for bad teeth

The big problem for ancient Egyptians in terms of oral hygiene was their diet. They ate a lot of bread, but they used stones to grind the flour, and pieces of grit and sand often ended up in the finished loaf! These ground down the teeth and wore away tooth enamel.

TEST OF TIME

Rotting teeth meant bad breath. To hide this, the Egyptians invented the first breath mints, made of cinnamon, myrrh, and frankincense, boiled with honey and shaped into lozenges. All over the world today, people suck mints to freshen their breath.

Picks and brushes

The Egyptians are also credited with inventing toothbrushes, although the Babylonians may have come up with the idea at about the same time. These ancient instruments were little more than twigs with the ends deliberately frayed, but they helped remove food from between the teeth to keep the mouth healthier. The Egyptians also used toothpicks to remove food from their teeth after eating a meal.

This wall painting shows a range of ancient Egyptian food, including bread, fruit, and different meats. This rich diet probably contributed to their tooth decay.

Queen Hatshepsut is thought to have died from an infection caused by an abscess after she had a tooth removed.

Making toothpaste

A key invention that helped the ancient Egyptians keep their mouths healthy was toothpaste. At first, they used ground-up ox hooves, burnt eggshells, ashes, and a volcanic rock called pumice, which created a slightly gritty paste that polished teeth and kept them clean. These were not tasty ingredients, though! It was only during the period of Roman rule that the Egyptians started making a nicer-flavored toothpaste out of salt, dried flowers, and mint.

COSMETICS

The ancient Egyptians took great pride in their appearance. Fine clothing, valuable jewelry, and carefully applied makeup were signs that someone was a member of Egyptian high society.

GENIUS ★
★ KEEPING UP APPEARANCES

All in the eyes

The Egyptians are believed to have invented eye makeup more than 4,000 years ago. It became a constant feature of their appearance. Their makeup was usually either black or green. Black was made from lead and green was made from copper or a green mineral called malachite. These were mixed with another mineral, called galena, to make a sort of paint.

This box contains ancient Egyptian cosmetics. The ancient Egyptians believed that makeup prevented disease, and both men and women wore it.

Wigs

Head lice could be a problem in ancient Egypt, so to keep them away people shaved their heads. To replace the hair they had lost, wealthy people wore wigs. These were woven from real hair and wool from sheep. They were set in shape using beeswax.

WOW!

Although most people wore wigs if they could afford them, priests remained bald, as it was felt they were kept pure this way. In fact, priests may have shaved their whole bodies.

Shaving implements

The ancient Egyptians also shaved their facial hair, and may have been responsible for creating the first razors. Ancient shaving instruments made from sharpened stones and set in wooden handles have been discovered in Egypt. Despite shaving, they also made fake beards from the same material as wigs. Pharaohs usually wore ceremonial beards. Even the female pharaoh Hatshepsut was sometimes depicted wearing beards in paintings and statues.

The shape of someone's beard indicated their social status. Pharaohs wore their beards with square ends.

TEST OF TIME

The Egyptians are credited with inventing the style of hand mirror still used today. These were made from metal such as bronze, which was polished to a high shine so users could see their reflection. The mirrors were often expensively decorated.

ancient Egyptian razor and mirror

GLOSSARY

abscess A fluid-filled infected area

abstract Something that does not take the shape or form of a real thing

antibacterial Describes a substance that can kill bacteria

architect A person who designs buildings

artifact An object of cultural or historical significance

Book of the Dead An ancient Egyptian text that contained spells to help a person reach the afterlife

cesarean section The procedure of delivering a baby through an incision in the abdomen

chaff The dry outer casing of seeds of cereal grains, such as wheat

civilization The stage of a human society, such as its culture and way of life

constellation A group or cluster of stars

counterweight A weight added to one end of an instrument to balance the weight at the other end

culture The beliefs and customs of a group of people

export To send goods for sale to a foreign area

flint A hard type of rock that can be chipped and shaped into sharp objects

furrow A long, narrow trench in which seeds are sown to grow crops in rows

gnomon An instrument on a shadow clock or sundial that casts a shadow

harvest To gather a crop

hieratic An Egyptian writing system that used joined-up symbols

hieroglyphics The ancient Egyptian system of picture writing

inundation The rising and spreading of water over an area of land

irrigation The process of bringing water to farmland in order to grow crops

offerings Gifts given to the gods as a form of worship or to ask for particular things

mallet A hammer with a large wooden head

mummification The process in which a dead body is preserved and prepared for burial

papyrus A tall, reed-like plant used to make paper

pharaoh A king or queen in ancient Egypt

pioneer Someone who does something that has never been done before

pith The spongy white tissue lining a stem or rind

preserve To keep something in its current state by preventing it from decaying

prosperous Wealthy and successful

prosthetic Describes an artificial body part made to replace a real one

quarry A deep pit from which stone and other materials are removed

recede To back away or drop in level

reservoir A place where water is collected and stored

ritual A religious ceremony in which actions are performed in a particular order

sacred Of deep religious importance

tuberculosis An infectious bacterial disease

TIMELINE

7000 B.C.E. People first begin to settle along the banks of the Nile

3500 B.C.E. Two kingdoms of Upper and Lower Egypt exist

3100 B.C.E. The kingdoms are united under King Narmer

2686 B.C.E. Start of the period known as the Old Kingdom

2050 B.C.E. Start of the Middle Kingdom

1567 B.C.E. Start of the New Kingdom

712 B.C.E. Late Period begins

30 B.C.E. Egypt comes under Roman control

INDEX

LEARNING MORE

Websites

www.dkfindout.com/us/history/ancient-egypt/

www.historyforkids.net/ancient-egypt.html

www.natgeokids.com/uk/discover/history/egypt/ten-facts-about-ancient-egypt/

Books

Bow, James. *Forensic Investigations of the Ancient Egyptians*. Crabtree Publishing, 2019.

Rodger, Ellen. *Ancient Egypt Inside Out.* Crabtree Publishing, 2017.

Roxburgh, Ellis. *The Egyptian Empire*. Wayland, 2017.